# RIDING THE WAVES OF GOD

# RIDING the WAVES of GOD

## JOYCE M. CREIGHTON

XULON PRESS

Xulon Press
2301 Lucien Way #415
Maitland, FL 32751
407.339.4217
www.xulonpress.com

© 2022 by Joyce M. Creighton

All rights reserved solely by the author. The author guarantees all contents are original and do not infringe upon the legal rights of any other person or work. No part of this book may be reproduced in any form without the permission of the author.

Due to the changing nature of the Internet, if there are any web addresses, links, or URLs included in this manuscript, these may have been altered and may no longer be accessible. The views and opinions shared in this book belong solely to the author and do not necessarily reflect those of the publisher. The publisher therefore disclaims responsibility for the views or opinions expressed within the work.

Unless otherwise indicated, Scripture quotations taken from the Holy Bible, New International Version (NIV). Copyright © 1973, 1978, 1984, 2011 by Biblica, Inc.™. Used by permission. All rights reserved.

Paperback ISBN-13: 978-1-6628-4884-1
Ebook ISBN-13: 978-1-6628-4885-8

# DEDICATION

First, I dedicate this book to my LORD and Savior Jesus Christ who has been with me my whole life. I thank and praise you.

I want to thank my husband who has been in heaven for the last twenty-three years. Jim, you brought me to my faith and will always love you.

To my beautiful and wonderful children Brandon and Heather. Thank you for always being there for me. I hope you know there is nothing I would not do for you. I will always love you.

I want to also dedicate this book to my grandchildren Erini and Nefeli. You two bring so much joy and love to Grandma. I will always love you.

To my daughter-in-law Nicole who is like a second daughter to me. Thanks for all you do for our family. You are so caring and giving.

One other person I dedicate this book to is Denise one of my best friends. I thank you for guiding me and teaching me more about Jesus every day.

To another best Friend Paula, who for forty years has been my guide to decision making and being there for me in good and bad.

To Nancy Schultz my church friend over twenty-six years. Thank you for taking me under your wings to be my mentor and teach me about Jesus Christ.

Finally, thanks to Kim Zierke, my church friend who has inspired me with her special Godly wisdom and believed in me enough to encourage me to write this book.

# RIDING THE WAVES OF GOD

As a child of GOD, I was baptized by the water and the word. Of course, at that time I had no idea why this was important to my parents.

**(WAVES) MATTHEW 28:19 (NIV) "Therefore go and make disciples of all nations, baptizing them in the name of the Father, and the Son, and the Holy Spirit."**

I grew up in a strict catholic home and was baptized in the Catholic Church. My three siblings and I had to go to confession every Saturday, and then go to church and receive holy communion on Sunday. I remember being scared to go into a confessional box to talk to a priest about how bad I was. I learned what a sin was but was fearful of the priest hearing them. This made me feel guilty. I also did not fully understand what a sin was but was scared to say them to a priest. This is when you made your communion at seven years old. Then there was the rule that you could not eat before receiving Holy Communion. I really did not understand all the things that were rules of the Catholic Church. I did what I was supposed to do to be Catholic. I did not grow up with a Bible in my house and I was terrified talking to a priest after a Sunday service because I thought they knew my sins because of the confessional box. In my late teens, I started questioning things about the catholic church. First there was the rule of wearing a hat on your head (but now you do not) Then you had to fast on Fridays with not eating meat. (Not anymore). One other thing was there are no more confessional boxes, but we confessed our sins together in a church service. What? This was confusing to me. Was this God changing these rituals? I was not sure. Church was my safe place so why would he make it confusing?

**(WAVES) ROMANS 12:2 (NIV)** "Do not conform to the pattern of the world but be transformed by the renewing of your mind. Then you will be able to test and approve what Jesus's will is-his good, pleasing, and perfect will."

# HIGH WAVES–I AM BLESSED WITH FRIENDS

*I*n my late twenties, I worked for this company where I ended up meeting several great people who have been my friends for over thirty years. There is Paula and Sue. There also was Al and Marianne who later disrupted my life. There was one more person. His name was Jim. Jim would talk with everyone every day. One day he called me and said," this is Jim Creighton would you like to go out with me?" I told him I would let him know. You see, there was a Jim Layton also who worked there. So, I had to ask my friends which one Jim Creighton was so that I could say the right thing. They told me which one Jim Creighton was and I was glad to go out with him. Well one date led to many, and two years later we got engaged. We were very much in love. When we started to plan a wedding, we realized we needed more money, so I found another better paying job. Then about six months later, Jim, also got a job at the same company. It was there I met another life- long friend. Her name is Deniese, who later became my best friend and number one mentor in learning about Jesus. Her and I would help each other with problems and victories. Deniese would quote scripture that pertained to the issue we were discussing to put GOD's perspective in my mind. It always made me look at my situations differently. One of the best phrases Deniese taught me is "Confusion is not of GOD." I have used this in helping make life decisions and still do. Deniese came from a troubled past and then later in life she met a gentleman who was living in the Word, and they ended up getting married. Then she became a woman of the Word and the two of them have been doing Christian music ministry for over twenty years. One of the best things Jesus did for me was send me both Jim and Deniese. Deniese moved to Colorado for her ministry which was devastating for me, but we have stayed connected every day, week etc. for over thirty years. Together we have walked in through good and tough times and helped each other as friends and in God's word. We remain best friends today. My belief is that one faithful friend is precious, and many faithful friends are a true blessing. I grew up liking everyone. Funny, I found out later this is what a Christian is supposed to do all the time. I am thankful for all my friends.

**(WAVES) JOHN 15 – 12:13 (NIV) "This is my commandment, that you love one another as I have loved you. Greater love has no one than this, that someone lay down his life for his friends."**

Jim and I continued to see each other every day and our love grew stronger for each other. I was twenty-six and he was thirty-five. We started to prepare for our wedding. Then, a couple of months into the planning, we hit a block in the road. You see, I was catholic, and Jim was Lutheran. Jim was married for a brief time once before, but by the court. I always thought church and state were separate, but it did not turn out that way. I wanted to get married in a church and my dad insisted I get married in the catholic church. The next step to solving this was to talk to a priest. First, we went to the church I grew up in and they told us we would have to do an annulment of Jim's previous marriage to get married in the catholic church. The annulment questions were exceptionally long and personal and it was going to cost about six-hundred dollars to get done. We went to four other churches and were told by each priest the same thing; you need to do the annulment. Every time we visited a priest, they interrogated Jim about his life, sex life, and parents. Also, each priest questioned Jim on his past. It was like he was being punished. I felt bad for him, and he was doing this for me. Jim knew a lot about the BIBLE. This did not matter. It was his personal history with love and intimacy that mattered to the priests.

My Dad could not understand this, so he said to go to his boyhood church and the church we went to on Sundays with my grandma. He told my mom to come with us. This time my mom went with us. My mom was in shock at the way they interrogated Jim. She and I left in tears. My dad could not believe how the priest could be this way to Jim but for some selfish reason of his own my dad would not come with us to visit a priest. However, we did start the annulment procedure, but we did not know if it would be done by the time, we would get married. This was a frustrating time, but Jim was born and baptized Lutheran' so we went to his boyhood church. They said they could marry us! My dad was happy I was getting married in a church. Hallelujah! felt good about the way it came out. This made my dad extremely happy so now we could relax and continue planning our wedding. I was more than, relieved. I felt like GOD was there to intervene. This also taught me to never ever give up on a dream!

**(WAVES) PHILLIPIANS 2:3 (NIV) "Do nothing out of selfish ambition, or vain conceit. Rather in humility, value others above yourself."**

# HIGH WAVE – GETTING MARRIED

Our wedding day finally came. It was a beautiful day! I remember the sun was shining most of the day. When I got to the church, there was my dad and mom standing proudly in the back. My dad had been using crutches to walk for about ten years due to having polio when he was younger. I believe GOD knew how much my dad wanted me to get married in the catholic church, because when it came time to walk me down the aisle, my father dropped his crutches and held on to me tight and managed to walk me down the aisle! I walked down this long aisle in complete tears; so much that I could not see my fiancé or the pastor. This was overwhelming that he did this for me. I was truly humbled! We did not practice this at rehearsal. I did not know he was going to do this. He just put his faith in Jesus at that moment. You see, he never walked without his crutches. He could not. Whatever faces I could see through my tears all had tears in their eyes too.

During the ceremony it rained for about ten minutes. When the ceremony was over, and we walked outside it was sunny. There is an old cliché that says, "when it rains on your wedding day it is good luck." The reception was happy and fun. It seemed like everyone was telling my dad what a beautiful service it was and that it was remarkably like a catholic ceremony. He was incredibly happy. Then it was time for the father-daughter dance. My dad met me on the dance floor and this time he handed his crutches to my mom. He grabbed me tight, and we did the father-daughter dance. This was only a temporary thing, but it was such blessing! Jesus had to be there, but I did not realize it at the time. A lot of people at the reception started to cry. Years later when I looked back on that day, I knew Jesus was there. Years later I looked back and remembered the rain and realized how good our marriage really was.

**(WAVES) ACTS 3:16 (NIV) "By faith in the name of Jesus, this man whom you see and know was made strong."**

# LOW WAVE – MISCARRIAGE

Things were going well since Jim and I both had good jobs, so in three years we were able to purchase our first home. This was because we both worked at the same company which was stable. We were doing great and had everything we needed. After two years in our first house, we started to plan to have children. I knew I wanted to have children since I was a little girl, so I was so excited when I became pregnant in our third year of marriage! During the last few weeks of my first trimester, I started having pain in my abdomen that kept getting worse and worse. I went to the doctor who immediately put me in the hospital. The pain was horrific! I was passing in and out. I was only in the hospital a couple of hours when I heard "get her into surgery!" All I remember is being rushed down the hallway into the operating room. I found out later that I almost died. Three days passed when I woke up from a coma. I remember waking up and seeing so many people in my room it looked like I woke up at my funeral. It was scary! I did not remember anything that happened or why I was there. I found out later I went thru an atopic pregnancy that burst; and my body filled up with poisonous gases. I was devasted! I lost the baby and one ovary, but happy I still was alive. I cried for days. This opened my eyes to learn even more about GOD. I kept thinking *"Why does GOD let these things happen?"* I asked my friend Deniese and she said, "Jesus does not these things happen. He has a plan for our lives and pain and suffering was not his plan. Also, I know Jesus doesn't give you more than you can handle." The only other thing I could think of was that <u>*"maybe something was seriously going to be wrong with this baby."*</u> I also had a challenging time dealing with the loss. This is where I had to start learning to trust Jesus. This loss hurt so bad that even when I would hold a baby or see couples in the store with a baby I would just start crying. This took about six months to get over.

**(WAVES) LUKE 8-48 (NIV) Then he said, "Daughter your faith has healed you; go in peace."**

We had been attending a Lutheran church in our area for a couple of years now and I had gotten to know the Pastor. I liked the church and the people, so it was the right time to take a class to learn about the Lutheran Missouri Synod beliefs so I could belong to a Lutheran church. This was on my mind since I married Jim, but the timing was never there. Jesus tapped me on the shoulder to let me know that now was the right time. I was extremely interested in learning more about the Lutheran Church Missouri Synod and the BIBLE. This is where I also realized why God brought me Jim. He was very inspirational to my faith since he knew the Bible and grew up Lutheran. One day while I was in this class, one of the first questions I asked the pastor is "what is the difference between a catholic priest and a pastor? Why can a Pastor be married but a Priest cannot?" The Pastor explained: "A Priest is married to GOD (which is why priests cannot get married). "A Priest is ordained to teach about GOD and his life and why he died for us." "A Pastor is ordained to teach about GOD and his life thru Jesus' WORD which is THE BIBLE. When we pray, we pray to GOD in both cases, but in the catholic church we have other people to teach GOD's Word, e.g., Bishops, Archbishops, and the Pope. In the Lutheran church we have a Pastor, who teaches GOD's word and GOD. I learned a lot about the word and Lutheran beliefs in this class. There is only one GOD, but everyone has different religious beliefs in worshipping that GOD. It was in this class I was handed my first BIBLE. My hands shook from excitement! I never had my own BIBLE being raised Catholic. My grandparents had a BIBLE. I had an uncle who was studying to be a priest and he sometimes read the BIBLE to us, but the only other BIBLE I saw was on the altar at the catholic church. Things are different now. I always read the BIBLE, and now I can refer to certain scriptures which pertain to what is happening in my life. After a six- week class, I became a member of OUR SAVIOR LUTHERAN CHURCH Missouri Synod. I could feel that my life would change. When I look back, this was meant to happen because GOD brought me Jim and Jim brought me to Jesus.

**(WAVES) THESSALONIANS 5:18 (NIV) "Give thanks in all circumstances for this is the will of GOD in Christ Jesus for you. Praise GOD."**

# HIGH WAVES-EXPECTING AGAIN

*E*ight months after my ectopic pregnancy, I was pregnant again. Praise God! The doctor's watched me very closely. I enjoyed this pregnancy including being sick because I did not know if it would I would be able to be pregnant again. I knew this baby was a gift from GOD. The pregnancy was easy and went fine. I had a beautiful and healthy baby boy. We named him Brandon. He was healthy and he was baptized in the Church. We had good jobs, good health, and a lovely place to live. Life was good in all ways, so in three years we planned our second child. However, we realized we needed a bigger home. We found a home in the same area where we were living, so we could stay in our church. While we were looking for this house, I was pregnant with my second child. This pregnancy went well again. GOD was with me! Four months after moving into this house I had a beautiful and healthy baby girl. We named her Heather. She was baptized in the church. Two years after she was born, we realized the bigger home we had bought had too many repair issues. We thought about moving again. I knew there was the inconvenience of showing the house and the packing, but we just could not see it any other way. When my daughter turned two, we started looking. We did find a house in the next town from us and remained at the same church. When we saw this house, we knew this was the "one." Finally! The one way we knew was the minute we saw it we felt a tap from GOD to take it. We fixed it up the way we wanted it. One special thing we added was something we both always loved. A fireplace! This was a beautiful addition. We had great neighbors and friends from church. The kids had great neighbor friends, including friends at church. We stayed in this house for quite a while. "Home is where the heart is."

**(WAVES) MATTHEW 27:25 (NIV)** "The rain came down, the streams rose, and the winds blew and beat against the house, yet it did not fall, because it had its foundation on a rock."

The kids went to Sunday school, in which I was also involved. The more I could learn by teaching, I could help my kids learn more. When my daughter was three the church started a pre-school that she started to attend. She made several Christian friends and my son attended Sunday School where he met Christian friends. My husband and I were blessed with having jobs at the same company for years. We did not buy a lot of unnecessary material things. In fact, we only had one brand new car in our whole marriage. We were happy spiritually, had good health, and a great family. When we started to approach year number ten at the company, we received a surprise. There was a nationwide downsizing of the company, and we were both let go. So, a wonderful forever home, beautiful healthy kids, and two unemployed parents. This was devasting, scary and stressful. Where do we start? I tried to look at everything through GOD's eyes. I kept thinking *"he will provide."* This was hard for me to believe at first, but I did not want to lose my faith. We struggled the first couple of months being on unemployment. We both worked hard to find good jobs.

**(WAVES) MATTHEW 6:25 (NIV)** "Therefore, I tell you, do not worry about your life, what you will eat or drink; or about your body about what you will wear. Is not life more than food, and the body more than clothes?"

# LOW WAVE-JOB LOSS

Three months went by, I was fortunate to find another job: but it was harder for my husband. Eight months went by, and my husband came to me with an idea of working for a friend. His name was Al. He was our best friend of ten years and was the CEO of a company about sixty miles away. We always spent the weekends at Al and Marianne's house. He was the best man at our wedding and my son's Godfather. I was against Jim doing this, due to the fact I always heard you should not work for a friend because it could cause your friendship to end. I also was not thrilled that Jim would have to commute sixty miles one way every day. He discussed it with Al, and it happened. Jim took a job and drove all that way to support us and keep us from losing our home. After about a year of working for Al things were going well, and he got a promotion. We decided to sell our home and move closer to where he was working. I decided to leave my job, because the place where we were moving to would be a cheaper place to live. I had my doubts about the move and not working, but I was going to be able to spend time with my kids. Once again, another move. Later, I realized this was our plan but not GOD's. We were going to leave our loving, content home; leaving good friends, our church and the kids were leaving their friends. This made me sad. We sold the house fast. This was very emotional for all of us. We moved into a rental home until we could find a home we liked. We were there for about eight months and then we received another surprise. The company my husband was working for was being bought out and he could be one of the first to be let go. Hey no problem, right? Unfortunately, Jim did get let go. This was devastating because his friend never told him this could happen. I was best friends with his wife for over ten years and she never said anything. They may not have known when Jim first started working there but as a CEO you know if there are talks. He could have given us a head start on what to do. How could best friends let their best friends sell their home and move their children to leave them high and dry.

# HIGH-WAVE -LEARNING FORGIVNESS

*T*his was unacceptable! I was very hurt and angry! All I saw was rage at this couple! We tried to reach them, but they would not return our calls. What I needed now more than anything was to trust in GOD. I just did not know where to start. The only thing I could think of was to move back to where we moved from; back to the friends, family, and the church in the same area we moved from. However, we did not have a lot of money left over from the sale of our home and we were moving back to a more expensive area. This was one of my first real touch trials of life since my atopic pregnancy. We got friends to help us move and we found a house to rent. We moved back close to our real friends and family, and we were welcomed back by our church friends but neither one of us had jobs. We were scared. It took all our strength to get this done. My husband was getting unemployment, but it was not enough. We had enough money left for two months' rent. I was lucky and found a part-time job immediately and four months late a full-time job in two months. Luck was not it. I know GOD had to be there. My husband found an excellent job in about four months. We were on our way to starting over again! The LORD teaches us to Love one another and to forgive but I just could not forgive this couple. It took me over ten years and a lot of understanding of GOD's word to do that. Praise GOD. I learned if you forgive that you will be forgiven too. By now you are wondering why I do not ask Jesus "Why me?" One of the most significant reasons is that I feel like it creates doubt in my faith.

(WAVES) PSALM 56 3:4 (NIV) "When I am afraid, I put my trust in you. In GOD, whose word I praise – in GOD I trust and am not afraid, what can mere mortals do to me?"

# HIGH WAVE-BUILDING A HOUSE

We rented for three years and due to the amount of rent it was hard to save and still did not have enough money to buy a house. It seemed like we started to go backwards again with expenses. One big reason we also had to wait was because of everything that happened us, our credit was bad, and we could not get approved for a mortgage. Finally, after the three years we found a special town where we could afford to build a house cheap because my husband was a Veteran. I was a little nervous because I always heard things always go wrong or things get delayed when you build a home, but this house was coming from GOD. We started to build in July, and it was to be ready in May the following year. We were all so excited. It seemed like every weekend we would visit the property to see how far it had come. I remember after the hole was dug and the cement was poured in the foundation we went and walked around it. It was surreal to me that this would be our home. I praised and thanked GOD for this new foundation. We felt good knowing we got this far.

**(WAVES) JEREMIAH 29:11 (NIV) "For I know the plans that I have for you declares the LORD, plans to prosper you and not to harm you, plans to give you hope, and a future."**

There were a couple delays though, such as there was a shortage of some wood needed which delayed the building a couple of weeks and then later the cabinets in the kitchen took a while to get. It was frustrating, but I kept thinking *"patience is a virtue."* This was where GOD wanted us. Finally, after thirteen months we drove by one day and there from the side of the road there were two sunbeams over our home. Two days later we got the call about the closing. Praise GOD! However, due to the house taking longer to build the interest rates went up. We were supposed to start at six-hundred dollars for a mortgage. We were starting with a nine-hundred-dollar mortgage! This was frightening! We were stunned! I kept thinking *"GOD will provide."* However, somehow, I was having a tough time believing it. We moved into this home and our Pastor came and blessed it. I felt much more confident about everything. Then GOD found me a better paying full-time. Praise GOD! After two years in our new house my husband found an excellent job working for the Post Office, so I got to do what I always wanted. I opened my own daycare because we had a lot of space to do this. Remember, I always loved kids and enjoyed taking care of them and teaching them things. I had five children that I took care of. I did this for a year and a half and then things changed where clients would come and go, and I needed a better steady income. I decided to go back to work in an office. I went back to the same company I left and was able to keep my seniority.

**(WAVES) PROVERBS 3:5 Trust in the LORD with all thine heart; and lean not unto thine own understanding.**

Life was looking good for five years and then another bomb hit us. My husband got injured at work. He sprained his foot; or so we thought. He went to the doctor, and they said it was tendonitis. He was ok for a couple of months, but his leg kept hurting. He stayed on medication, but I could not get him to do more tests. After about six months he was still in pain. We talked about him going for more tests and he told me if he went, he would end up in the hospital and die. He went on to say he did not want to die in a hospital bed. We talked several times before about what would happen if something did happen to him regarding money. He would say he was worth more to me being dead because of his life insurance. Six months later, he got to the point of him limping. One night he got up in excruciating pain several times. I wanted to call an ambulance, but he did not want me too. The fourth time he got up he collapsed, so I got him in the car and took him to the hospital. When we got him to the hospital one doctor was talking about gangrene. Thich meant his foot was turning black. I could not believe what I was hearing! They did a doppler test because they thought he had a blood clot; but also, blood flow to his foot was extremely poor. Yes, he was admitted to the hospital. The first thing they did was cut his leg open and let it air to see if the clot would decrease. Then two days they had to do a leg surgery to try and find the clot that way.

**(WAVES) DEUTERONOMY 31:6 "Be strong and courageous. Do not be afraid or terrified because of them, for the LORD your GOD goes with you; he will never leave you nor forsake you."**

After two weeks the foot was not getting any better. His foot was getting to the point of too much blood loss. It was looking like he may be having the foot amputated I was very frustrated and confused. Then after a while I remembered one thing my best friend Deniese taught me when she went into ministry and that was "GOD is not of confusion. It is Satan that likes to confuse us." They tried one more thing which was a vein bypass. This is taking the good veins in the leg and thigh and bypassing them down to the foot. This was a nine-hour surgery. It was exceptionally long and stressful waiting for this surgery to be done. I read the BIBLE, talked with a couple of relatives. I prayed the whole time. The surgery was nine hours, but I never thought of Jim dying. He made it through! So, I told myself to trust in GOD and not the devil. As it says in the BIBLE in Romans 15:3, "suffering produces perseverance and perseverance produces character and character produces hope." I had to keep a positive attitude. I found out after the surgery he had only two good veins left in that foot. They waited a couple of days and discovered this surgery did not work with helping circulation. They wanted to amputate the foot! He was scared, nervous and on heavy drugs. I was scared too because this was the fourth surgery in three weeks. Could Jim make it threw another? I did not know it at the time, but my faith was being tested. They did the amputation, and it went fine. I went home when he got to his room so he could rest. That night he called me groggy, and in pain to tell me "I Love You."

**(WAVES) ROMANS 12:12(NIV) "Be joyful in hope, patient in affliction, faithful in prayer."**

# LOW WAVE-DEATH

The next day I went back to work. I had been taking time off and going to hospital when needed. I was at work only a half hour and I received a phone call from the hospital; it was the chaplain of the hospital. What? Chaplain? He said my husband took a turn for the worse. I ran out got in my car and started driving home. I worked forty miles from home. I do not even remember how I drove home. All the way home I Kept thinking *"maybe he went into a coma, and I could talk him out of it."* I stopped at school and picked up my children because I did not know what was going on. We got to the hospital floor and the elevator doors opened and there was my pastor. He said, "I'm sorry he didn't make it. "We walked into the room and there was Jim lying deceased. They kept oxygen flowing because he was an organ donor. I immediately jumped to him and started crying and kept hugging and kissing him! I did not want to stop. Then I had my children do the same. In a split second it seemed cruel to ask my children to hug their deceased dad, but I knew they had to do it for closure. All in tears they did it. This was like a scene from a movie a horror movie! Then a few minutes later an aunt and uncle of mine were coming to visit him, and they were in shock. It was chaos in the hospital room and then nurse kept pushing me to sign an autopsy form. Amid my tears and confusion somehow, I remembered my dad saying unless it is necessary, do not do an autopsy on anyone. You see, my dad's job was assisting pathologists in doing autopsies and he believed you should be buried with everything GOD gave us. I talked to the nurse, and she said they were changing my husband's bed and they sat him in a chair. Then he fell to the floor. A blood clot went to his lung. This gave me comfort know that he did not die in a hospital bed. This was good enough for me. No autopsy was done. A pulmonary embolism or blood clot was the cause of his death. Some of my friends and Jim's family came to the hospital and we all went to my house to start planning funeral arrangements. I was in a fog. I was a widow at age forty-six. This just could not be real. I was so confused. Then I remembered again, "confusion is <u>not</u> of GOD."

**(WAVES) THESSALONIANS 14:14 (NIV) "For we believe that Jesus died and rose again and so we believe that GOD will bring with Jesus those who have fallen asleep in him."**

It was a week before the funeral, so relatives could come in from out of town. Remember my best friend Deniese, well she and her husband came and stayed with me. I had friends from church, my kids' friends' parents, and relatives in and out for a week. This was a lot but when I look back very necessary. The help of my good friends from the church and my kids' friends' parents talking with us and making meals was a blessing! One other thing I had to do was to call our insurance agent and let him know. He was like a brother to us. He knew we always struggled with money. Well, he was at a conference on the east coast when he heard of Jim's passing and drove home to bring me my insurance checks. I did not care about the money I wanted Jim back. This was the first time in my life I was mad at Jesus and had to find a way get over it. I finally asked the dreaded question, "what I did wrong for you to take my husband?"

The day of the visitation came. This was a very painful and sad day. I cried from the moment I arrived till the time I left. The flowers were overwhelming. The people were too. You see, Jim always said he had no friends, but I stood in front of his casket crying and greeting people for six hours. If you remember earlier, I said that Jim thought he had no friends–well there were around two hundred friends and relatives that came to say good-by.

**(WAVES) GENESIS: 3:19 (NIV) "By the sweat of your brow, you will eat until you return to the ground, since from it you were taken; for dust you are and to dust you shall return. "**

The next day was the funeral service. Jim was moved from the funeral home to the back of the church we belonged to for last minute viewers. We walked into the service behind the casket. The church was full. It was a beautiful ceremony. During the service I stood up in front of Jim's casket and the congregation and thanked Jim for all he had given to his family, our life together and how he took care of our family. Jim always had a smile on his face. After the funeral and luncheon, we went back to our house and had a celebration in honor of Jim because this is what he would have wanted. My church friends and children's friends' and their parents came by and brought us meals and to check on us for several weeks after the funeral. We were blessed!

When people started slowing down to come around, I felt my grief more. I would hear the garage door open and close (or so I thought) and run to see him coming home from work. Every room I would go in was a memory. This went on for over a year. I went to a grief support group at our church. I would sit and cry every night for about a year. Grief does not just come and go. However, it is necessary for our healing. I was grieving, so much I spent two years getting his medical records from every doctor. Oh, I trusted in the LORD and believed there is a time to be born and a time to die, but I had a tough time with denial. I figured by getting his records and an attorney I could find blame with the doctors for his death. This became too stressful and took time. After two years I came to terms that it was his time to go and accepted reality.

LOW WAVE-DEATH

**(WAVES) ESCCLESIASTES 3:2 (NIV)** "There is a time to be born and a time to die."

I took a couple of months off work to get situated to a new life. I had to be a little more available for the kids. They went for counseling as well. I thank God for my children in so many ways but in this incident because they were and thirteen and sixteen when Jim passed, so I had to continue to go out and be with people even though I did not feel like it. I went to their school functions and church activities. This was a wonderful way to be part of life again.

**(WAVES) JERIMIAH 29:11 (NIV)** "For I know the plans I have for you."

As time passes grief does get better. When my son graduated wo years after my husband's passing it was very emotional. While at the graduation ceremony, I looked across the arena and saw a bright light shining on an empty chair. I had to acknowledge that it was Jim. He was there! It was an emotional but momentous day. Then my next loss came when my son went off to college. I felt like the two most important men in my life left me. Also, my son had seizures, and he now was living alone in an apt. He was on medication, but I prayed every night for his safety. Once a parent you are always a parent. I would worry about him having a seizure in the shower and falling. He did have a few "episodes," here and there but thanks be to GOD he was safe.

Riding The Waves of God

**(WAVES) MATTHEW 7:25 (NIV)** "Therefore I tell you do not worry about your life, what you will eat or drink; or about your body, what you will wear. Is not life more than food, and the body mor than clothes?"

Two years after my husband passed, I fractured my hip. I had emergency surgery and was laid up for about two months. I was frustrated but never asked GOD "Why me?" These words were not meant for me. They brought fear to me. I had my children and my friends to help me get through this.

I was able to get to work and out. I was just in a little pain and healed quite quickly.

**(WAVES) ROMANS: 5:3 (NIV)** "Not only so, but we also glory in our sufferings because we know that sufferings produce perseverance, perseverance, character, and character hope."

I was getting along smoothly, and then two years after I broke my hip, I was in a bad car accident. I was going to work on the highway and just as I approached the ramp for me to get off the traffic stopped. The next thing I knew my car was spinning around. I heard no tires screeching. My car spun at least three times and I was hit again by another car and pushed into the next lane. The next thing I knew I was stopped, and my body was frozen. I could not move. My eyes were open, so I just looked up to the sky and said, "Please LORD let me live." I did not realize how bad my injuries were. Suddenly a lady appeared at my window, touched my hand, and said, "I'm a nurse don't move." Later I found out if I moved, I could have been paralyzed. This mini truck hit me at sixty-five miles per hour broke my seat into my back and crushed three vertebrae. A few minutes later a big firefighter came through the passenger side of my car and had a white sheet and was going to cover my face. I was scared and said, "Don't cover my face I'm not dead." He was doing this cause due to my injuries they had to saw my door off to get me out of the car and the sheet was for protection. I was taken to the nearest hospital which turned out to be a nightmare. The pain was unbearable, and I was immediately put into a body cast. My blood pressure was so high they could not operate; So, after a week I was brought to my own hospital. The only thing I could do was lay straight and try to eat lying down. Thy did not want me to move. I had to wait three weeks before I could have a surgery because of my blood pressure. I laid as still as I could all that time. I was on some heavy meds and even with that there was pain, frustration, and discomfort. I just prayed day and night. I had people from my church come to the hospital and pray for me. I just kept looking up and praying and through the hospital ceiling knowing GOD was up there begged for my life. Surely, I would not want to give up and leave my children with no parents.

**(WAVES) JOB1-21 (NIV) Then he fell to the ground in worship. "Naked I come from my mother's womb, and naked I will depart." The LORD gave and the Lord has taken away." May the name of the Lord be praised."**

While in the hospital my attorney came several times. I asked the attorney if there was a women's name on the accident report. There were a few witnesses but no women. I could not understand. I explained to him about the women who appeared at my window after the accident. I was incredibly surprised because why would a woman who said she was a nurse stop to help but not leave her name. However, about five years later at a BIBLE Study I mentioned my story about the missing women and my leader explained that it was my guardian angel. I felt her touch me and I heard her speak, and she saved my life by telling me not to move! This was a big powerful moment in my faith for me!

The surgery had to be done at a special hospital about one-hundred and fifty miles away. After three weeks it was time to go to that special hospital, so I was put in an ambulance and taken there. **ALLELUIA!** I was feeling good with pain medication and happy I was finally going to have surgery. GOD got me this far so there was no giving up. I remember though, as I just arrived at that special hospital. Deniese called like five minutes later and prayed with me and read scriptures from the BIBLE. This was super encouraging and gave me more hope. I was to have the surgery in the next few days. I remember thinking the night before to be strong and that *"this is all in GOD's hands,"* but at this point it was hard to believe. When they took me down for surgery, I prayed all the way and when the anesthesiologist came to speak to me, I was really scared but had to and did believe Jesus will help me through this. I made the doctor tape a picture of my children and my favorite cross to the bed during the surgery. This was a six-hour surgery. When I woke up later, my children and my family were there for me. I just cried because I was alive! Thank you, Jesus!

**(WAVES) PSALM 40 vs.1:3 (NIV) "I waited patiently for the LORD. He turned to me and heard my cry. He lifted me out of the slimy pit, out of the mud and mire. He set my feet on a rock and gave me a firm place to stand."**

I was in the hospital for six weeks in a body cast and then rehab for eight weeks. I was on so much morphine I did not know what day or time it was for several weeks. The doctors were amazed! They kept saying because of the severity of my injuries, I should not have even been here. I had to learn to do things all over again; like brush my teeth, walk, sit, and wash and my hair. I had to wear a brace for three more months. It was six months before I was normal. I did not want to drive. That took about a year. This tragedy taught me two things: Trust in the Lord, and never get upset over trivial things. To this day these are mottos I live by.

I think by now you might be thinking wow this poor girl. Well yes and no. I was feeling very frustrated at this point but remember – perseverance brings character, and character brings hope.

Things were going smoothly for quite a few years aw then I decided to sell the house my husband and I built together because it was getting harder for me to take care of. I needed to downsize. This was an incredibly sad and stressful time for my children and myself. Saying good-by to our family home. When we built it part of the deal was, if we painted the house ourselves and we would save thousands of dollars. So, we spent a month painting railing, shutters, walls, and the whole outside and inside of the house. I remember my son at thirteen, rolling paint in his bedroom and my ten-year-old daughter rolling paint on her wall. These were only a preview of all our memories. The day we moved We all cried. I cried as I walked through each room one more time.

My daughter and I moved to a smaller home in the next town. She left after a couple of years later and moved out of state. A few years after moving to that house I broke my foot and crushed my ankle. Yes, Jesus is still evaluating me. I was coming home from being out with a friend and she dropped me off. It was winter and as I was walking to my front door, suddenly, I heard my bone break on my left leg. I mean I HEARD the bone break. The next thing I knew I was on the ground. I did not have my phone with me, so I laid in the snow crying and screaming for help. I realized no one would hear me cause all windows were closed. I prayed for help. I loo ked down and saw my broken leg and started crawling to the door. The only way I was able to get into the house was by crawling and dragging my broken foot beside me. I would stretch my hand in the snow and used my good knee to crawl. Every time I had to crawl which was about six times I would cry out "Please Jesus help me. "I trust You." I crawled about eight-hundred yards, managed to get to the phone and call the paramedics. A friend came right when the ambulance arrived. I had immediate surgery. My tibia and fibular bones were broken, and I crushed my ankle. While in the ambulance I realized who helped me get to the door that night. It was Jesus! Later I found out that this happened because of lack of calcium. You see, when I was going through my grief of the loss of my husband, I was also going thru the change of life. I did not take my calcium like I was supposed to. This made my bones become more brittle.

**(WAVES) PHILLIPPIANS 4:13 (NIV)" I can do all things through him who gives me strength."**

    I was in a wheelchair for a while and then therapy. This was a very painful accident. My daughter and my friends and my church friends once again was there for me. I did not give up on the healing. I was in a cast for a while but still able to make it to work. All things do get better. Or do they?

    Six years went by, and I was at my cousin's summer home in Wisconsin. We went for dinner and then came home and went to sleep. This was a big home and normally I slept upstairs in a bedroom. This night after we got home, I fell asleep on the couch downstairs Sometime in the middle of the night, I guess, I was going to the bathroom and started walking up the stairs. The next thing I remember was seeing my robe swirling around me and then I heard a voice. It was my cousin calling my name. I had fallen down the stairs by tripping on my robe and fell back and hit my neck on a wrought iron chair. I was out of it. I cracked a vertebra in my neck. The irony of this story is that not even ten feet away from where I was sleeping downstairs, there was a bathroom, and I did not need to go up the stairs. However, I ended up in the hospital for a week and rehab for a month. I have to say this was a difficult one for me. I had a brace on my neck day and night and to avoid surgery I could not move my neck at all. If I jerked it a certain way, I may have had to have surgery. This brought a lot of fear to me because I did not want that surgery. I lost a lot of sleep because I was afraid to move while I slept.

**(WAVES) PSALM 119:28 (NIV) "My soul is weary with sorrow. Strengthen me according to your word."**

I could not work for a couple of years. The house myself and my daughter were living in kept falling apart and I could no longer afford the mortgage. After a year and a half, I had to walk away and take a loss on the house. My daughter got married so I found a low- income facility to move into. This would help me save and get back on my feet. A few months after I moved into the apartment, I found a fantastic job. GOD always provides and he provided me with one of the most rewarding jobs ever. I went to work at a Senior Center!

The next five years were so good to me. This job of working with and helping seniors, made me realize how blessed I was to survive all the things I went through. I felt a peace. Then one day I happened to be undressing in front of a mirror and found something that looked weird on one of my breasts. I went to the doctor. I had a mammogram. I always kept up with my mammograms so there should not be any problems. They also did an MRI. The next day I got the call to come in. It was Cancer! I have survived a lot of pain in my life… but the C word is the most awful word to hear. They did another breast scan and during this scan I listened to the words of the song "IN THE EYE OF THE STORM, by Ryan Erickson. This is a song of hope and how GOD is in control. This was my cancer song. I listened to it on all the bad days. Immediately I looked up to the LORD and prayed. "Please don't let it be bad. You are a healing GOD." They set me up right away with an oncologist. She told me I was going on stage three breast cancer. I was terrified! She explained this would require surgery, chemo, and radiation. I asked for a referral to one of the better hospitals in the Midwest to see a surgeon. GOD certainly hears prayers, because when I met the surgeon, and she explained every detail felt as if I was talking to one of his angels. I had surgery in less than a month. This was one scary surgery too. I had stage three breast cancer and it was in most of my lymph nodes. I had a mastectomy and all lymph nodes had to be removed. I was in the hospital for three days. I had no idea what recovery was like until I went through it. They got all the cancer. I am a believer in Christ, but it took all my inner strength to get through every day. I had six months of chemo and radiation. Whenever I had a chemo treatment, I had my daughter or close friend go with me. This encouraged me to want to live. I did not feel like I was getting a treatment. I kept all positive thoughts. I also looked at pictures of my kids and grandkids to keep me positive. This was for Hope, and it reminded me why I was getting chemo. The days I felt bad I rested as much as I could. I read scriptures from the BIBLE. I would watch funny movies. When I felt down, I called a friend or got up and tried to do something small around the house to keep going. When I had energy, I had to keep moving and live. I also knew my healing came from the LORD. JESUS was my rock and strength. My family and friends were all part of my healing process. It is five years later, and I am still cancer free. Praise GOD! I continue to work part-time, go to an exercise class, and help other seniors now. Thank you, Jesus for my life.

**(WAVES) LUKE 8:48. Daughter your faith has healed you. Go in peace.**

Life is like a wave. There are many ups and down. How you look at that wave is what really matters. The ocean is his and he blesses it. Ride the wave and because Jesus is always with always with you!

# LAST PAGE

*I*n my life, I had more blessings than obstacles, even though after reading this book it would seem the opposite. Life is precious. In Romans 3:23 it says, "For all have sinned and fall short of the glory of GOD."

Jesus gave us a beautiful thing, Salvation, grace, forgiveness, and the right to eternal life. By him dying we live. Everyday should be a blessing and new mornings bring new mercies in health, sickness, pandemics, and family problems. Jesus is always there.

They say as you get older you get wiser, but you also get more grateful. I am grateful you read this book.

Remember: Jesus said, "I will never leave or forsake you." Isaiah 55 8:9" For my thoughts are not your thoughts, neither are your ways my ways, declares the LORD. For as the heavens are higher than the earth, so are my ways higher than your ways and my thoughts than yours."

In conclusion: John 14:27 Peace I leave with you: my peace I give you. I do not give to you as the world gives. Do not let your hearts be troubled and do not be afraid.

# RIDING THE WAVES OF GOD

This book is not an autobiography in the sense that it does not have "all" things that took place in my life. I wanted to write this book to let others know how when life throws us curves, what we can do. When we go thru life, we have many experiences. There are some of us who have all good; and some have not so good experiences. We also make changes in our lives that help us. We hope these changes are always better and more productive for our lives; however, sometimes that is not true. Also, we have changes we have no control over. I know in my life many changes were not of my free will and they disrupted my life. Whenever I was able to be at the ocean I was always amazed at its power. I would listen to the sounds and watch the waves. I would notice big waves little waves and then some high and some lower. Then they roll and disperse in different patterns. This reminded me so much of my life on the "ups" and downs" Whenever I had some of these "unwanted" changes, watching the waves gave me comfort. This picture of calm and knowing GOD created the ocean led me to the title of my book.

Whether you are a Christian or not, or living with constant pain, mental struggles or everything is always fine, there is someone there "riding those waves with you."

CPSIA information can be obtained
at www.ICGtesting.com
Printed in the USA
LVHW010044210922
728862LV00013B/495